Map Reading Puz...

Teacher's Book

by Carol Matchett
Pupil's Book by Jenny Alexander

Contents

Section 1: for Below Average Readers
Guided reading and writing lessons using:
"Where's My New CD?"

Teaching Notes for Guided Reading	2
Teaching Notes for Guided Writing	3
Copymaster 1: labelling features	4
Copymaster 2: writing instructions	5

Guided reading and writing lessons using:
Running on Empty and *The Disappearing Dinner*

Teaching Notes for Guided Reading	6
Teaching Notes for Guided Writing	7
Copymaster 3: comparing instructional texts	8
Copymaster 4: writing instructions	9

Section 2: for Average Readers
Guided reading and writing lessons using:
Dodgy Dave and Nina the Knife

Teaching Notes for Guided Reading	10
Teaching Notes for Guided Writing	11
Copymaster 5: identifying different types of text	12
Copymaster 6: writing instructions	13

Guided reading and writing lessons using:
Searching for Sweets and *The Newsman's Nose*

Teaching Notes for Guided Reading	14
Teaching Notes for Guided Writing	15
Copymaster 7: evaluating instructions	16
Copymaster 8: editing instructions	17

Section 3: for Above Average Readers
Guided reading and writing lessons using:
Escape from the Evil Regent

Teaching Notes for Guided Reading	18
Teaching Notes for Guided Writing	19
Copymaster 9: evaluating instructions	20
Copymaster 10: writing instructions	21

Guided reading and writing lessons using:
On the Trail of the Siberian Rubythroat

Teaching Notes for Guided Reading	22
Teaching Notes for Guided Writing	23
Copymaster 11: evaluating instructions	24
Copymaster 12: writing instructions	25

Edinburgh Gate
Harlow, Essex

Map Reading Puzzles — Year 5 Term 1 — Section 1 Below Average Level

"Where's My New CD?"

Guided Reading

Key Objectives
- Read instructional texts identifying purpose, organisation and layout features.
- Revise work on verbs.

Each child will need a set of labels from **Copymaster 1**, an overhead transparency sheet and non-permanent pen. A pencil and paper will be needed when solving the puzzle.

Introduction
- Read the book title and invite the children to skim through the puzzles. *What sorts of puzzles can you see? How will you solve them?*
- Read the introduction to 'Where's My New CD?' as far as 'Follow the directions to find out where the CD is hidden.' *What is the purpose of the puzzle? How do you solve it? Where does the writer tell you this?*
- Use this discussion to establish the instructional nature of the text. Identify instructions that:
  1 tell the reader what to do ['look at the plan']
  2 state what will be achieved ['find out where the CD is hidden']
  3 provide directions for the reader to follow in order to achieve this goal ['start at the gate'].
- Ask the children to read the directions and follow them on the plan opposite.

Reading and Discussion
- Monitor the children as they read and follow the directions. Check their use of scale and compass points.
- They should then continue to read and follow the instructions on page 4.
- As children finish, they should check their answer as instructed in the text and then look through the other puzzles in the book.
- Discuss the puzzle on page 4. *What was the purpose of doing this puzzle? Where does the writer tell you this? How did you know what to do? What part of the text told you this?*
- Evaluate how easy/difficult the children found the two puzzles.
- Discuss how the directions were set out to make them easy to follow. [Numbered steps; a clear, ordered list.]
- Give out the labels from **Copymaster 1**. Read through them. Discuss any unfamiliar terms. Ask the children to place the labels on pages 2 and 3 to identify the features used. Discuss the features used/not used. *Why isn't there a list of items needed?*
- Repeat with page 4. *Why aren't numbers used in these instructions?*
- Turn back to the directions on page 2. Give out the overhead transparencies. Ask the children to underline the verb/s in each step. Check the identification of verbs. Discuss the position of verbs at the start of each sentence. Explain that this makes the instructions sound direct, like orders.

Returning to the Text for Evaluation and Analysis
- Reinforce the terms, instructions and directions. *What is the purpose of instructions and directions?* [Instructions tell you what to do and directions tell you how to reach a particular destination.]
- Ask the children to describe typical features of instructional texts that were identified during the session, including the position of verbs.

© Pearson Education Limited 2003

"Where's My New CD?"

Guided Writing

Key Objective
- Write instructional texts and test them out.

Task
Use **Copymaster 2** to help write a puzzle based on the guided reading text. Test it out.

Each child will need **Copymaster 2** and *Map Reading Puzzles*.

Introduction

- Briefly discuss the puzzles read in guided reading. Focus on the text type and purpose. *How did you solve the puzzles?* [By following the instructions/directions.]

- Give out the copies of **Copymaster 2** and introduce the task. *We are going to write our own puzzle and then test it out.*

- Read through **Copymaster 2**. *What parts of the puzzle do you need to write?* [**1** the instructions to tell the reader what to do; **2** the directions to locate the football; **3** the grid references to help the reader check their answer.]

- Turn to page 3 of the guided reading text. Suggest possible hiding places for the football. Ask each of the children to select a hiding place – but make sure they don't tell the other members of the group.

- Discuss how to complete the initial instructions to the reader. *What should you tell them? Remember to start with the verb – it sounds more like an instruction or a command, for example, 'Follow …', 'Read …'.* Ask the children to rehearse the sentence orally before they begin writing.

Children Writing Individually

- As the children write, encourage them to reread their own work. *Check that your instructions and directions are clear. Have you started with a verb?*

- Remind the children to set out the directions around the garden as a numbered list. *This will make it easier for your reader to follow.*

- Encourage reference to compass points and to the scale to help make the directions precise. *Tell your reader how many steps, and in what direction.*

- In the final section of the copymaster, remind the children to set out their grid references clearly. *Remember the order is very important. Make sure it is clear to your reader.*

Evaluation

- Ask the children to swap their puzzles with a partner. *Try out your partner's puzzle. If their instructions are clear, you should be able to solve the puzzle and check the answer.*

- *If you have any difficulties, remember what the problem was, and be ready to tell your partner how to solve it.*

- When the puzzles have been tested, encourage the children to evaluate each other's work. *Were the instructions easy to follow? How did the layout help? Were there any problems?*

Suggested Independent Activities

- Use the **Copymaster 1** labels to analyse other examples of instructional texts.
- Draw a plan of the classroom. Write a treasure hunt puzzle for the rest of the class.
- Collect examples of directions/puzzles.

© Pearson Education Limited 2003

Features of Instructional Texts

Cut out these labels.

- tells you the purpose at the start
- gives a list of items needed
- gives an ordered list of steps to be taken
- uses numbers to make the order clear
- diagram
- plan
- map
- labels
- scale
- grid
- key
- other feature

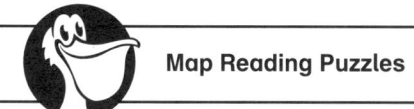 Map Reading Puzzles    Copymaster 2   "Where's My New CD?"

Writing Instructions for a Puzzle

Write your own puzzle.

"Where's My Football?"

To get her own back, Leah hides her little brother's football. If you can find it, you might just stop a major fight!

Look at the plan of Leah's garden, on page 2. _____
_____

1 Start at _____
_____
_____
_____
_____
_____

Where was the football? Find out if you were right from the alphabet grid on page 4.

You will need _____

Write _____

Give your puzzle to a friend. Let them test it out.

© Pearson Education Limited 2003

Map Reading Puzzles   Year 5 Term 1   Section 1 Below Average Level

Running on Empty and The Disappearing Dinner

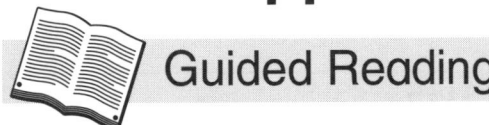
Guided Reading

Key Objective
◆ Read and evaluate two instructional texts in terms of their purpose, organisation and layout, and clarity.

Each pair of children will need Copymaster ❸ and a set of labels from Copymaster ❶.
The teacher will need an enlarged copy of Copymaster ❸.

Introduction

◆ Explain the purpose of the session – to follow and compare two sets of instructions.

◆ Show the enlarged Copymaster ❸ and read the headings. *This is how we will make our comparisons.*

◆ Read page 5 to the children. Ask them to skim pages 6 and 7. *What is the purpose of these instructions? What will you find out?* [The shortest distance/who was right.]

◆ Read the first paragraph on page 9. *What is the purpose of following these instructions?* [To find the location of the alien's dinner.]

◆ Record the purpose of each text on the enlarged copymaster.

◆ Give out the labels from Copymaster ❶. Explain that these are the instructional text features the children should be looking for and recording on the copymaster.

◆ Put the children into pairs and give out the copymasters. Ask some pairs to read 'Running on Empty' first and some to begin with 'The Disappearing Dinner'.

Reading and Discussion

◆ Monitor the children as they read and follow the instructions. Check how successfully they apply the instructions to the maps to complete the activity.

◆ Encourage the children to analyse any problems they have. *Why are you not sure? What is making it difficult? Is there something you don't understand?* Remind the children to record their comments on the comparison table.

◆ Use the labels to encourage discussion of the instructional features used in the text and illustrations.

◆ When the pairs finish the first puzzle they should be directed to go straight on to the second. [If time is short, ask the children to just skim through the second puzzle and read it in full later.]

◆ Make sure each pair has discussed and completed the comparison chart.

◆ Bring the group back together. Compare the instructional features used in each text. *Why do you think the writer numbered the points on page 6? Why is a list of items needed on page 6, but not on page 9?*

◆ Invite the children to comment on how clear/confusing they found the instructions. *What problems did you have? What did you find helpful?*

◆ Compare the maps. *Which was the easiest to follow? Why?*

Returning to the Text for Evaluation and Analysis

◆ Ask the children to draw conclusions and come to an overall evaluation of the two sets of instructions. *Which were the clearest/easiest to follow? Why?*

◆ Encourage the children to support their evaluations by referring to key features, e.g. instructional text features, the types of map used, and/or the language of the text.

© Pearson Education Limited 2003

Map Reading Puzzles Year 5 Term 1 Section ❶ Below Average Level

The Disappearing Dinner

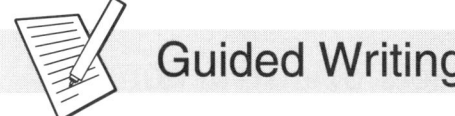
Guided Writing

Key Objective
◆ Use the imperative form of verbs in instructional writing and the past tense in recounts.

Task
Write the recount given on **Copymaster ❹** as an instructional text.

Each child will need **Copymaster ❹** and paper or a notebook for writing. The teacher will need a whiteboard and marker pen and an enlarged set of labels from **Copymaster ❶**.

Introduction

◆ Briefly discuss the guided reading text 'The Disappearing Dinner'. *What was the puzzle about? What did you have to do?*

◆ Give out copies of **Copymaster ❹**. Introduce the task by reading the instructions at the top of the page. Focus on the purpose. *The instructions will tell the reader how to have the perfect holiday on Zura. This is made clear by the heading/title.*

◆ Ask the children to write the heading at the top of their paper.

◆ Read the recount aloud. *Does this sound like a set of instructions? Why not?* Through discussion, establish that the recount describes what the alien did, rather than telling people what they should do.

◆ On the board, write the sentence 'First, I found a good place to land.' *How can we make this into an instruction?* Focus on changing the verb, replacing 'I found' with 'find'. Read the sentence back. *Now it sounds like an instruction, because the verb is telling the reader what to do.*

◆ Use the labels to discuss how the instructions might be organised, e.g. list of items needed, sequence of steps, possibly numbered. Display these on the board.

Children Writing Individually

◆ Suggest the children begin their writing by making a list of items needed.

◆ Remind the children to set out their sequence of steps in a way that makes them easy to follow, e.g. using a separate line for each step.

◆ Observe how the children change the verbs from past tense to imperative form. Encourage them to rehearse the sentences aloud before they write them down. *Does that sound like an instruction?*

◆ Ensure that children change pronouns, i.e. replacing the word 'my' with 'your'. Stop the group and draw attention to this if necessary.

Evaluation

◆ Ask the children to swap their work with another member of the group. *Check your partner's work. Have they changed all of the verbs correctly? Is it set out like a set of instructions?*

◆ Identify examples of irregular verbs used in the writing, e.g. 'find/found'.

Suggested Independent Activities

◆ Draw a labelled map to accompany the new set of instructions.

◆ Use a road map to compare distances between towns. Write instructions describing the process.

◆ Collect different sorts of instructions.

© Pearson Education Limited 2003

Comparing Instructional Texts

Complete this table to help you compare two sets of instructions.

	Running on Empty (pages 6 and 7)	**The Disappearing Dinner** (pages 9 and 10)
The purpose		
Instructional features		
Comments on the instructions *(Were they easy to follow? Why? What was difficult?)*		
Comments on the map *(Was it easy to follow? Why? What was difficult?)*		

Recount to Instructional Text

Here, an alien recounts how he had a perfect holiday on the planet Zura. Change this recount into a set of instructions called **'How to have a perfect holiday on the planet Zura'**.

I have just had a perfect holiday on the planet Zura. You should try it.

I took with me all of the things I needed. I had my swamp-suit, my star-glasses and of course my spaceship.

First, I found a good place to land. I brought the spaceship down gently on a flat part of the planet.

Then, I climbed out of the spaceship and made straight for the gloopswamp. I changed into my swamp suit and enjoyed a good wallow.

After a few space hours, I left the gloopswamp. It was time to explore the planet. I returned to my spaceship and left my swamp-suit to dry.

I headed towards the singing stones and listened to them for a while. Then I carried on towards the litebrite pool. I put on my star-glasses to protect my eyes. I walked round the edge of the litebrite pool and went towards the glowing ferns.

At dinner time, I made my way back to my spaceship.

 Map Reading Puzzles   Year 5 Term 1   Section ❷   Average Level

Dodgy Dave and Nina the Knife

 Guided Reading

Key Objectives

- Read and evaluate an instructional text.
- Revise work on verb tenses and verb forms in relation to purpose of text.

Each child will need Copymaster ❺.

Introduction

- Read the title of the book and invite the children to skim through the pages. *What sort of book is this? What will we have to do? Have you done puzzles or used maps like these before?*
- Find the first page of 'Dodgy Dave and Nina the Knife'. Read the opening paragraph to the children. *What is the purpose of this information?* [It sets the scene by providing background information about the characters.]
- Ask the children to read the rest of the 'scene setting' on page 11. *What else does the 'scene setting' tell us?* [It describes the events in the getaway.] *Is it written like a story/narrative?* [There are similarities, e.g. the sequence of events, but it is written in the present tense rather than the past tense.] Establish that it is more like a commentary, describing the events as they happen.
- Read the instructions at the top of page 12. *What is the purpose of the puzzle? What do we have to do?* [Establish that the purpose is to locate the money on the map by following the directions.]
- Look at the map. Make sure the children are familiar with the key and the symbols used.
- *The directions are in a speech bubble. They are written as if Dave is speaking them – one after another. When you read and follow Dave's instructions, you will need to break them up into small steps, otherwise there will be too much to remember.*

Reading and Discussion

- Monitor the children as they read and follow the directions. Check they break the text up into a sequence of smaller steps.
- Make sure they use the symbols on the map to identify landmarks mentioned in the text, e.g. 'pub', 'main road'. *How do the landmarks help you to follow the instructions?* [You can check you're on the right road.]
- Clarify the meaning of any technical map reading terms, e.g. 'fork'.
- The children should read page 14 to check their answer.
- Bring the group back together. Focus on the different types of text featured. *What type of text is featured on page 14? Compare to pages 11 and 12.*
- Give out Copymaster ❺. Ask the children to complete the labels and underline the verbs as instructed.
- Discuss the verb tense/forms used: present tense in the commentary; imperatives in the directions; past tense in the newspaper recount.

Returning to the Text for Evaluation and Analysis

- Reinforce that the type of verb used relates to the purpose of the text.
- Ask the children to evaluate the directions given by Dodgy Dave. *Did you find them easy to follow? Were they clear? What problems did you have? What helped you?*

© Pearson Education Limited 2003

Map Reading Puzzles Year 5 Term 1 Section ❷ Average Level

Dodgy Dave and Nina the Knife

 Guided Writing

Key Objective
- Use the imperative form in instructional writing and the past tense in recounts.

Task
Use the commentary provided on **Copymaster ❻** to write directions for the police car chasing Dave and Nina. Write a police report recounting the incident.

Each child will need Copymaster ❻, the map in *Map Reading Puzzles* and a notebook or whiteboard and marker pen.

Introduction
- Review the three types of text featured in guided reading. [A newspaper report, directions, and 'scene setting' commentary.] Focus on the purpose and verb forms, e.g. a newspaper report recounts events that have already happened and uses past tense.
- Give out **Copymaster ❻** and explain the task. Establish the purpose of the two forms of writing: the directions give instructions to the chasing police car; the police report provides an official recount of the events.
- Read the commentary aloud, making it sound authentic. Ask the children to follow the route on the map.
- Reread the commentary a sentence at a time. Ask the children to rehearse orally the instructions to be given to the chasing police car. Ensure use of imperative forms.
- Ask the children to write the instructions in their notebooks or on their whiteboards. *Remember to use the imperative form.*

Children Writing Individually
- When writing the directions, encourage the children to include more detail for the chasing police car, e.g. by including references to landmarks ['past the pub'].
- *Read your instructions to a partner. Are they written in the imperative form? Do they sound like orders?*
- Stop the group before they write the police report. Read the opening suggested on the copymaster. Use this to establish important points, e.g. the use of past tense to describe what happened; the inclusion of time connecting phrases, e.g. 'at 11.33'.
- You may also want to discuss the use of formal/official language, e.g. 'as instructed', 'believed to be'. Discuss other possibilities and encourage the children to use these when writing, e.g. 'proceeded', 'continued'.

Evaluation
- Read aloud samples taken from the group's written directions and police reports. *Can you identify the form? How can you tell?*
- Which was easiest/most successful?
- *How were the two pieces of writing different?* Reinforce the differences in purpose, use of verbs and choice of language.

Suggested Independent Activities
- Use a map of the area around the school. Write directions for a partner to follow.
- Write a recount of a familiar journey. Swap with a partner. Write directions based on your partner's recount.

© Pearson Education Limited 2003

Verbs in Different Types of Text

Complete these labels to show the different types of text. Underline the verbs or verb chains in each example.

Dave and Nina crash their car on Albert Bridge. Nina hides under the bridge. Dave grabs the money and runs. When he is too tired to run any more, he dumps the bag of money over a wall and goes back to look for Nina.	**Introduction/commentary** **Purpose:**
Stay on the main road until it crosses a track. Turn left up the track. When you come to a choice of tracks, take the left fork. Keep going until you come to a lane. Turn left. That brings you onto a minor road. Go straight across.	**Directions** **Purpose:**
Nina Watson was caught today with a holdall full of stolen money. A man raised the alarm when he saw someone behaving suspiciously in the cemetery in old Windsor.	**Newspaper report** **Purpose:**

Writing in Different Forms

The police helicopter is following Dodgy Dave and Nina the Knife as they make a getaway. Here is part of the helicopter pilot's commentary back to base.

They are heading towards Old Windsor on the main road …

They are crossing the river at Albert Bridge …

… turning left at Manor Farm roundabout …

… they are staying on the main road …

Now they're taking a sharp left past the car park …

1 Write the directions for the chasing police car.

Car 00B3 here are your directions

Head towards …

2 Write the police report of the car chase.

Date of incident:

Details of incident: At 11.33 we were instructed to follow a car believed to be the getaway vehicle of Dodgy Dave and Nina the Knife.

As instructed, we headed towards Old Windsor on the main road …

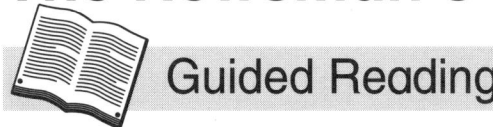

Map Reading Puzzles | Year 5 Term 1 | Section ❷ | Average Level

Searching for Sweets and The Newsman's Nose

Guided Reading

Key Objective
- Read and evaluate instructional texts in terms of their purpose, organisation, clarity and usefulness.

Each pair of children will need Copymaster ❼ and an overhead transparency sheet and non-permanent pen.

Introduction
- Explain that in this session the children will read and solve a series of map reading puzzles by following directions.
- Introduce the purpose of the session: to evaluate the directions given. *When evaluating, you should think about how the directions are organised, whether they are clear and how useful they are in helping you solve the puzzle.*
- Give out the copies of Copymaster ❼ and explain the star rating system.
- Point out that the 'Comments' section can also refer to features of the maps and plans that the children found useful/or that caused difficulty.
- Put the children into pairs. *One of you will read the instructions; one will follow the route on the map/plan using the overhead transparency sheet. Take it in turns to read/mark the route.*
- Read the scene setting introduction on page 15 to the children. Point out the speech bubble on page 16 and establish the purpose. *Who is giving these instructions? Who to? Why?*
- Remind the 'reader' to break up the sequence of instructions into steps or stages to make it easier for their partner to follow.

Reading and Discussion
- Observe the children as they read and follow the directions.
- Use questioning to encourage each pair to analyse the directions for clarity and usefulness. *Why are you uncertain? What is the problem? Were the directions easy to follow? Why? What helped?*
- As they finish each puzzle, the children should discuss the star rating with their partner, and record comments on the copymaster.
- Repeat the process for each puzzle in the guided reading text.
- At an appropriate point, stop the group to make comparisons between the directions on page 16 and those on page 20. *Which did you find easier? Why?*
- Focus on the technical language used in the directions on page 20. *Did you understand the terms 'T-junction', 'obelisk', 'bears right'?*
- Compare using the plan of Poshe Hall and the map of Balmoral. *Which was easier to use? Why? Did you understand the symbols on the map?*

Returning to the Text for Evaluation and Analysis
- Encourage each pair to offer an overall evaluation of the directions read. *Which were the easier/harder? Why? Which would be most suitable for younger children? Why?*
- Focus on the use of detail to make the directions clear. Ask the children to locate examples of detail in the text, e.g. 'Turn right before you get to the entrance hall'; 'When the road turns sharply to the right …' *How does the extra detail help?*

© Pearson Education Limited 2003

Map Reading Puzzles   Year 5 Term 1   Section ❷   Average Level

Searching for Sweets and The Newsman's Nose

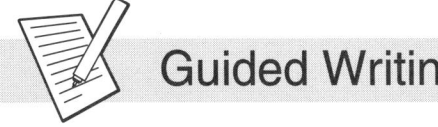

Guided Writing

Key Objectives
- Write instructional texts and test them out.
- Revise and edit writing to improve clarity.

Task
Revise and improve the instructions given on **Copymaster ❽**. Write own instructions, paying particular attention to clarity.

Each child will need **Copymaster ❽** and *Map Reading Puzzles*.
The teacher will need a whiteboard and marker pen.

Introduction

- Before the session begins, write these phrases on the board: 'when you get to', 'at the', 'you will see', 'stop before', 'between', 'as far as', 'towards', 'pass', 'through'.
- Discuss the directions read in the guided reading session. *What helped to make directions easy to follow?* Establish the importance of detail to guide the reader.
- Give out copies of **Copymaster ❽**. Ask the children to find the map on page 17 of the guided reading text. Read the directions provided on the copymaster. *Are these easy to follow? What is the problem?* Establish that there is not enough detail; they leave the reader uncertain about where to turn.
- Introduce the task. On the board, write the sentence: 'Go out of the blue room.' *Could this be clearer?* Read through the words and phrases on the board. Add to the original sentence, e.g. 'You will see a long corridor.'

Children Writing Individually

- Ask the children to make this change on the copymaster and then continue to revise the rest of the directions.
- Encourage the children to use the words and phrases from the board to add more detail.
- Use discussion to help the children decide what information the reader needs to know, e.g.: *How will the reader know when to turn? How will they know they are in the right corridor?*
- Point out that phrases such as 'when you reach the dining room', can be placed before or after the instruction to 'turn right'.
- When the children have revised the given set of directions, they should begin to write their own set of directions as instructed on the copymaster. [A different map or plan can be used if preferred.]
- Remind the children to think about the needs of the reader. *Give detail about exactly where they should turn, how far they should go, etc.*

Evaluation

- Ask the children to swap their directions with a partner to test them out.
- Encourage the children to evaluate each other's work. *If you have any difficulties, tell your partner where they need to make the instructions clearer.*

Suggested Independent Activities

- Make a plan of the school. Write instructions describing how to reach various locations from your classroom.
- Write directions to accompany an Ordnance Survey map of the local area.

© Pearson Education Limited 2003

Map Reading Puzzles — Copymaster 7 — Searching for Sweets and The Newsman's Nose

Evaluating Instructional Texts

Give each set of instructions a star rating.

Write comments to explain your decision.

Key
**** very clear
*** quite clear
** a little confusing
* very confusing

Instructions on page 16
Star rating:

Comments (*What helped/caused problems?*)

Instructions on page 18
Star rating:

Comments (*What helped/caused problems?*)

Instructions on page 20
Star rating:

Comments (*What helped/caused problems?*)

Instructions on page 22
Star rating:

Comments (*What helped/caused problems?*)

© Pearson Education Limited 2003

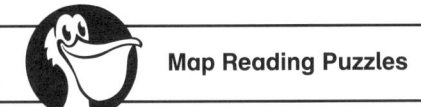 Map Reading Puzzles  Copymaster 8   Searching for Sweets and The Newsman's Nose

Editing Instructions to Improve Clarity

These instructions refer to the plan of Poshe Hall on page 17. They describe the route from the blue room to the study, but they are not very clear. Can you improve them?

How to get from the blue room to the study

Go out of the blue room.

Turn right.

Turn left.

Turn left again.

Turn right.

Turn right.

You're at the study.

Now write your own directions.

How to get from _____ to _____

(17)

© Pearson Education Limited 2003

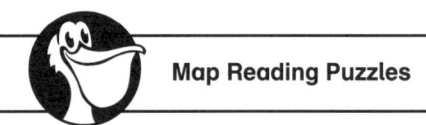

Map Reading Puzzles   Year 5 Term 1   Section ❸ Above Average Level

Escape from the Evil Regent

Key Objective
- Read and evaluate an instructional text in terms of purpose, clarity and usefulness.

Each pair of children will need an overhead transparency sheet and non-permanent pen, and Copymaster ❾.

Introduction

- Read the title of the book and invite the children to skim through the pages. Encourage predictions of the content. *What will you have to do to solve the puzzles?*

- Find the guided reading text and discuss the title. Use the glossary to clarify the meaning of the word 'regent'.

- Read page 23 aloud in a suitably dramatic voice. Encourage the children to make predictions about the puzzle before turning the page. Use the discussion to focus on instructional texts and to introduce the objective for the session. *What must you do to escape? Why is it important that the instructions are clear?*

- Turn the page and look at the map on page 25. Identify the features described in the last paragraph on page 23. Discuss the labels, compass and symbols. *How will each of these help us to follow Mazarin's instructions?*

- Put the children into pairs. *One of you will read the instructions on page 24; one will follow the route on the map using the overhead transparency sheet. Swap roles when you get to page 26. Think about whether Mazarin's instructions are clear and helpful.*

- Explain that the 'reader' will need to separate out the instructions into a sequence of steps, to give their partner time to find and follow the route.

Reading and Discussion

- Watch the children as they read and follow the instructions. Monitor whether the reader breaks up the instructions into sensible steps, e.g. *Make sure you read the warnings before it's too late.*

- Use questioning to encourage the children to evaluate the instructions. *What helped you to follow the route? How did you know to go this way?*

- Remind the children to swap roles on page 26 and repeat the process.

- Encourage the children to give their evaluation of the instructions. *Were they easy/difficult to follow? Why?* Encourage the children to refer to details given in the text or maps to support their evaluations.

- Give out the copies of **Copymaster ❾**. Read Mazarin's advice on giving accurate instructions. Ask the children to go back through the text and identify examples of each feature. Record these on the copymaster.

- Discuss the importance of giving precise information that guides the reader accurately, e.g. *Why are the warnings important? Why are references to landmarks useful?*

Returning to the Text for Evaluation and Analysis

- Ask the children to give an overall evaluation of Mazarin's instructions. *Did they lead you to safety? If you went wrong, why?*

- Consider the points made on the copymaster. *Did Mazarin follow his own advice? How did this help to make the instructions clear?*

© Pearson Education Limited 2003

Map Reading Puzzles — Year 5 Term 1 — Section ❸ Above Average Level

Escape from the Evil Regent

Guided Writing

Key Objectives
- Write instructional texts and test them out.
- Use imperative form of verbs in instructional writing.

Task
Use the recount provided on **Copymaster ❿** to write the instructions given by Mazarin to escape from the castle of Santora.

Each child will need **Copymaster ❿**, *Map Reading Puzzles* and paper for writing.
The teacher will need an enlarged copy of **Copymaster ❾**.

Introduction
- Briefly discuss the purpose of Mazarin's instructions in the guided reading text.
- Introduce the purpose of the writing session by developing the story further. *Some of your followers were not so lucky. They were captured by the evil King of Santora and imprisoned in his castle. Luckily Mazarin was able to get instructions to them and they were able to escape.*
- Give out **Copymaster ❿**. Explain that this recounts the first part of their escape. Read the recount and introduce the task. *You will write the instructions sent by Mazarin that helped them escape.*
- Discuss the differences between a recount and instructions, e.g. a recount describes events that have happened [using past tense], instructions tell the reader what they should do [using imperative verbs].
- Use the enlarged copy of **Copymaster ❾** to revise Mazarin's key points about giving accurate instructions. *Follow this advice to make sure the instructions are clear.*
- Discuss how Mazarin's instructions might start, e.g. by stating the purpose ['Follow these instructions and you will escape safely …'], listing equipment ['You will need a torch …'].

Children Writing Individually
- The children begin writing the instructions following the recount.
- Check the use of imperatives, e.g. 'Find the entrance …', 'Press the lever …'
- The children should refer to the map on page 26 to help them complete the instructions. *These people will only be safe when they reach the beach. What directions will Mazarin give?*

Evaluation
- *Swap instructions with a partner. Start at the point where you come out of the tunnel. Follow the rest of the instructions on the map. Are the instructions successful?*
- Discuss whether appropriate directions, distances, warnings have been given.
- Introduce the task of completing the recount based on the instructions they have written. *How will the recount be different?* [Using past tense verbs.] Set this as an independent activity.

Suggested Independent Activities
- Make the instructions look like an old document.
- Use Mazarin's advice to write directions around the school/local area.
- Collect instructions for games/puzzles.

© Pearson Education Limited 2003

 **Map Reading Puzzles** **Copymaster 9** **Escape from The Evil Regent**

Giving Accurate Directions

The magician Mazarin offers this advice on giving accurate directions. Can you find examples in the directions he gives on pages 24 and 26?

Make the direction of travel clear. They must know which way to go.

Then head South ...

Give distances. Tell them how far they need to go and when to stop.

Follow it until the first sharp bend.

Give warnings – particularly if there is a danger that they might go the wrong way.

Don't go over the bridge.

Refer to landmarks. This will help them be sure they are on the right track.

It comes out near the bridge to Bonemelt Island.

© Pearson Education Limited 2003

Map Reading Puzzles   Copymaster 10   Escape from The Evil Regent

Giving Directions – Which Way Now?

Write instructions for the escape from Santora castle based on this recount.

Escape from the Castle of Santora

We found the entrance to the underground passage hidden behind the tapestry in the Great Hall. The door was locked, but as we pressed the lever to the right of the fireplace it slid open. Remembering to close the door behind us, we entered the passageway.

We were glad we had brought a torch, because once inside it was completely dark. Using the light from the torch we were able to follow the tunnel gently downhill as it took us underground and beneath the walls of the castle.

After about ten minutes we came to a place where the passageway divided, just as Mazarin had told us. Remembering his warning about the danger that lurked in the tunnel to the left, we quickly took the right hand fork.

Almost immediately the passageway took a sharp bend to the right and we could see light ahead of us. We made our way quickly towards the light. When we came out into the open we found ourselves at the northeast corner of the castle. The sinister mountains of Morg were directly ahead of us ...

© Pearson Education Limited 2003

Map Reading Puzzles Year 5 Term 1 Section ❸ Above Average Level

On the Trail of the Siberian Rubythroat

Guided Reading

Key Objectives
- Read and evaluate instructional texts in terms of purpose, organisation, clarity and usefulness.
- Discuss the purpose of note-making and nature of notes made.

Each child will need *Map Reading Puzzles*, paper and a pencil.

Introduction

- Before the session begins, prepare the guided reading texts by covering the map on page 29 with a piece of card.
- Read the title and ask the children to read the opening paragraph of the guided reading text. *What is the purpose of the directions that follow?*
- Ask the children to read and complete the puzzle on page 27. *Make a note of the route taken on the paper.*
- Allow a few minutes for the children to complete the activity then discuss the instructions and the notes. *Was it easy/difficult to follow the instructions? Why? How did you record the route?* Compare different ways of noting the route, e.g. a list of places, using arrows, key phrases.
- Introduce the dual purpose of the session:
  1 to evaluate instructions
  2 to make notes for different purposes.
- Ask the children to turn to pages 28 and 29. *The map has been covered. This means you will not be able to see the instructions and the map at the same time. Will you be able to remember the instructions given by the bird warden? What could you do to help you remember?* [Make notes.]
- Ask the children to read the instructions given on page 28 and to make appropriate notes.

Reading and Discussion

- Monitor the children as they read and make notes. Make sure they do not simply copy out the bird warden's instructions. Suggest note-making techniques, e.g. key words, lists, bullet points. Discuss the amount of detail necessary.
- When the children have made their notes they can uncover the map. The card should now be used to cover the instructions printed on page 28. *Follow the route on the map, using your notes to guide you.*
- Discuss the activity, evaluating both the instructions given by the warden and the children's own note-making. *Did you find the right place? Were the instructions clear? Was the map easy to use? Was your note-making clear?*
- Read and complete the puzzle on page 30. Evaluate the instructions.
- Ask the children to imagine they were sending a message to a fellow bird-watcher, directing them to the Pechora Pipit. *Write instructions from the landing strip. Use no more than 20 words in your directions.*
- *Was this activity difficult? What words did you need to include?*

Returning to the Text for Evaluation and Analysis

- Ask the children to evaluate the three puzzles. *Were the directions clear and useful? Explain your evaluation?*
- Discuss the different purposes of note-making used in the session [to record, as a reminder, to instruct], and the different note-making techniques used.

© Pearson Education Limited 2003

 Map Reading Puzzles Year 5 Term 1 Section ❸ Above Average Level

On the Trail of the Siberian Rubythroat

 Guided Writing

Key Objectives
- Write instructional texts, and test them out.
- Discuss and edit their own writing for clarity.

Task
Write a guide for bird watchers visiting Fair Isle that gives directions to the best viewing sites.

Each child will need a copy of **Copymaster ⑫** and paper for planning.
The teacher will need an enlarged copy of **Copymaster ⑪**.

Introduction
- Introduce the task. Make clear the purpose [to provide useful directions] and the audience [visitors to the Fair Isle].
- Give out copies of **Copymaster ⑫**. Read through the information provided. Explain that the map will be included in the guide to help illustrate the directions.
- Discuss what directions to include in the guide, e.g. from the bird observatory to each site, or directions for a tour of the island including visits to all the sites.
- Discuss how the directions might be organised. *What have you learned about writing instructions from your reading?*
- Show the enlarged copy of **Copymaster ⑪**. Refer to the features listed to discuss ideas for the organisation and layout. *Will you need to list any items needed?* [Possibly include a list of useful items, e.g. binoculars, waterproof coat.] *Will sub-headings be useful?* [For example, to separate directions to each site.]
- Tell the children that they are going to make a first draft of the guide in this session. The final version will be presented later.

Children Writing Individually
- The children should begin by writing their heading and/or opening sentence. *This should make the purpose of the guide clear.*
- Ask the children to explain how they are going to proceed, e.g. including a list of useful items, using a sub-heading such as 'How to reach site 1'.
- As the children write, refer to the points made on **Copymaster ⑪** about clarity and layout. *Have you given enough detail? Will the reader be confused? Is it better to separate out the directions?*
- At a suitable point ask the children to work with a partner to check their work for clarity. *See if you can follow your partner's instructions. Identify anything that is not clear, or that doesn't sound right. How can it be improved?*
- Allow the children time to make any changes/improvements to their work.

Evaluation
- *Were your instructions clear? What improvements have you made after discussing your work? What was the hardest part to get right?*
- Evaluate whether the group needs a further guided writing session, or whether they can continue this work as an independent activity.

Suggested Independent Activities
- Present the bird watcher's guide as an information leaflet.
- Use **Copymaster ⑪** to evaluate other instructional texts.
- Write a map reading puzzle based on a local Ordnance Survey map.

© Pearson Education Limited 2003

Map Reading Puzzles   Copymaster 11   On the Trail of the Siberian Rubythroat

Evaluating Instructional Texts

Use these guidelines to help you evaluate instructional texts. You can use the same guidelines to help you evaluate instructions that you write yourself.

Feature	Comment
Purpose: is the purpose made clear at the start? *Is the purpose clearly stated in the heading or opening sentence?*	
Organisation: are the instructions well organised? *Are the steps needed clear and ordered? Are any of the items needed listed before the main instructions begin? If the instructions are very long, are they divided into sections?*	
Layout: does the layout help the reader follow the instructions? *Are diagrams, pictures, maps used? Are lists of points numbered, or are letters or bullet points used? Are sub-headings used if needed?*	
Clarity: are the instructions clear at all times? *Are details given about what, how, where, when? Does the writer provide additional information to avoid confusion?*	
Usefulness: were the instructions useful? *Did they help you to achieve the goal/purpose? Were they suitable for you to use – or were they aimed at someone older/younger?*	

© Pearson Education Limited 2003